Travis Bradberry and Jean Greave's

Emotional Intelligence 2.0

Study Guide

BookCaps™ Study Guide
www.bookcaps.com

Table of Contents

Disclaimer

BookCap Study Guides™ are not officially endorsed by the publisher or author of the book.

Historical Context

TalentSmart® is Travis Bradberry and Jean Greaves's emotional intelligence training, consulting, and testing agency that administers the *Emotional Intelligence Appraisal®* test. Their position as leaders in the field has given them the chance to observe the progress of hundreds of thousands of individuals at all career levels. In addition, they have taken an interest in the patterns and shifts in larger EQ trends, such as overall implications for health, happiness, career success, and earnings potential; differences and similarities between the generations and the sexes; and the influence of culture.

According to the authors, the notion of emotional intelligence began to gain ground when people realized that IQ could not by itself account for professional success or earnings. After the idea was featured on the cover of *Time* magazine and on television, interest in the subject burgeoned. Numerous books came out, including Bradberry and Greaves's *The Emotional Intelligence Quick Book*, which has since been sold worldwide in more than twenty languages. However, despite training hundreds of people a week in how to improve their EQ, they realized that the demand for learning and understanding emotional intelligence had far outpaced the available resources, so they decided to fill the need by writing *Emotional Intelligence 2.0.*

Aside from being a best-selling author, Travis Bradberry holds two Ph.D.s from the California School of Professional Psychology, one in clinical and one in industrial/organizational psychology. He is a regular speaker at top companies and the co-founder and president of TalentSmart®, the global leader in emotional intelligence testing and training. Co-author Jean Greaves, who is the co-founder and CEO of TalentSmart®, likewise earned her Ph.D. in Industrial/Organizational Psychology from the California School of Professional Psychology. Her background is in workforce development and healthcare consulting, and her skills include emotional intelligence training as well as public speaking, with an additional focus on leadership development.

Plot Summary

One of the fundamental observations of Travis Bradberry and Jean Greaves's book *Emotional Intelligence 2.0* is that IQ, education, and knowledge alone are not the determining factors of success but that success is more often correlated with what is called "emotional intelligence." The problem that arises is that although the idea of emotional intelligence resonates with a lot of people, no one seems to know just what it is or that it can be learned and improved. Bradberry and Greaves's book can help us understand its nature and practical manifestation, its effect on our lives, and its role as a self-management tool with the ability to increase our capacity for success.

It is only fitting that the book's first chapter begins with a true story illustrating emotional intelligence (as well as the lack of it) in action. Butch Connor's confrontation with a great white shark had an intensity that few of us will ever experience. But that day Butch learned something about his, mind, body and emotions: once he realized that his emotions were governing his body counterproductively, he used his reason to reverse the process—and it worked. He had discovered one of the essential elements of emotional intelligence—the ability to manage his emotions rather than letting them manage him.

Unlike IQ, which Bradberry and Greaves claim to be a fixed learning capacity, EQ can be developed. To this end, the book presents 66 strategies together with an assessment test, both of which are part of a program designed to maximize emotional intelligence in a way that is tailored to each individual. The assessment test, which is strongly recommended, acts as summary of current individual skills, a learning guide, a memory aid, and a means of measuring progress.

In Chapter 2, the authors describe the bigger picture of emotional intelligence before examining the details of the different strategies. They make us aware of the sheer range of our emotions, their different categories and intensities, types of problems typically encountered, the definition of a whole person, and the link between EQ and success.

In Chapter 3, we learn of the four basic skills that constitute EQ: self-awareness, self-management, social awareness, and relationship management. The chapter focuses on general definitions and case studies so that we can get a sense of what each skill looks like in practice.

Chapter 4 begins by explaining the value of developing our EQ and then introduces us to the Emotional Intelligence Action Plan. Chapters 5 through 8 outline the specific strategies for each of the four skills and the Epilogue summarizes different trends in emotional intelligence and their implications for our world.

The authors' goal in writing the book was to give as many people as possible the chance to understand and hone their emotional intelligence skills. Just as entire cultures benefit from the cultivation of emotional intelligence, so, too, can individuals, companies, families, and other groups. But the authors warn that EQ skills need to be actively maintained—that they can decline as well as improve and that those who neglect to actively cultivate them run the risk of decreasing their overall quality of life—economically, personally, and professionally. However, those who do take up the challenge to explore and improve this facet of human intelligence will find their own lives and the lives of those around them benefited in multiple ways.

Key Concepts

Emotional Intelligence (EQ)

EQ is divided into two main categories: personal and social competence, which are in turn divided into awareness and management. Together, these constitute the four main skills of emotional intelligence: self-awareness, self-management, social awareness, and relationship management. Until recently, EQ has always been eclipsed by IQ, which was thought to be the crucial factor in determining success. Yet studies have revealed that a high IQ accounts for only 20 percent of successes while a high EQ explains an impressive 70 percent. Unlike IQ, though, which Bradberry and Greaves claim to be a static learning capacity, EQ can be developed.

The Whole Person

The authors distinguish three main aspects of the person: IQ, EQ, and personality. They define IQ as the fundamental ability to learn that remains the same throughout an individual's lifetime. Unlike IQ, EQ can be improved through learning and practice, although some people come by it more naturally than others. Furthermore, there is no correlation between IQ and EQ, which are considered entirely separate skills. The same holds true for personality which, like IQ, is deemed unchanging and separate from emotional intelligence. Personality can be used to help improve EQ, but like IQ, it is not essential to the process. Taken together, they give a more complete picture of the whole person.

Triggers and Hijackings

The authors define "emotional hijackings" as those instances when our emotions get the better of our thinking and take over our actions, often to our detriment. "Trigger events," on the other hand, are those events that produce an extended emotional response. The range of possible emotions is extensive, but according to Bradberry and Greaves, they can all be categorized under five main headings: happiness, sadness, anger, fear, and shame. These are further divided into high, medium, and low degrees of intensity. On any given day, we typically experience many different specific emotions at varying levels of intensity, yet a lack of emotional awareness plagues two-thirds of the world's people, who are unable to either identify, comprehend, or manage their own emotions.

Self-Awareness

As the name suggests, "self-awareness" means being aware of and understanding your own positive and negative emotions and reactions. It entails being willing to honestly work through both your feelings and whatever triggers them. In fact, according to the authors, just thinking about self-awareness helps to improve the skill, and because it is such a basic aspect of emotional intelligence, a well-developed self-awareness improves a person's abilities with the other three EQ skills as wells. Finally, being aware of oneself makes an enormous difference in both overall personal satisfaction and job performance and so should be applied to every aspect of our lives.

Self-Management

Self-management refers to the action or restraint that results from self-awareness. It is the ability to steer your life in a positive direction, whether that means managing stressful situations or dealing effectively with temporary uncertainty. An important characteristic of self-management is the ability to defer momentary needs or desires in favor of a larger goal. Those who can do this are more likely to achieve their goals while at the same time maintaining their emotional balance. The ability to manage your emotions won't turn your life into a fairy tale, and there will still be trigger moments, but on the whole, you will experience much more control over your life.

Social Awareness

Like self-awareness, social awareness is what the authors call a "foundational skill," a skill that provides the basis for developing other abilities. It is the awareness or accurate perception and understanding of other people's thoughts and emotions, involving the ability to pick up on cues through such aspects as body language, facial expression, and tone of voice. In other words, it is the ability to key into people's emotions, and it has been found to be remarkably consistent across different cultures. To do so requires being both present and clear as well as having an outwardly directed focus that enables you to imagine another person's or group's feelings without allowing your own preconceptions to interfere.

Relationship Management

Relationship management can be viewed as the culmination all four skills because it utilizes the previous three to effectively manage interactions and relationships. Bradberry and Greaves differentiate between "relationships" and "interactions" according to their frequency—the more frequent the interaction, the more it turns into a relationship. They emphasize the need to manage all interactions, including the difficult or unpleasant ones, since doing so generally enhances genuine communication and aids in resolving conflict and stress. Not least, they see quality relationships as an important aspect of life, something to be cultivated and valued, but at the same time, they recommend adopting the attitude of finding worth in every interaction.

The Emotional Intelligence Action Plan

The Emotional Intelligence Action Plan combines the use of a test designed by Bradberry and Greaves, called the *Emotional Intelligence Appraisal,* with 66 strategies aimed at strengthening the neural pathways that connect the emotional and rational parts of the brain. Using the test as a starting point, the process involves focusing on one skill at a time along with three carefully selected strategies related to that skill. Participants are encouraged to work with a mentor or guide adept in the particular skill and to spend three to six months practicing the new habits before repeating the process for the next skill. Through these deliberate changes in thought and behavior, the brain's "plasticity" allows it to gradually add connections, so that what once was a struggle eventually becomes habitual.

Trends in Emotional Intelligence

Having tested, trained, and studied hundreds of thousands of cases all over the world, Bradberry and Greaves have observed several different trends in emotional intelligence:

- *Overall US trends*—In a five-year US study from 2003 to 2007, Bradberry and Greaves observed a steady upward trend in both average worker EQ and the number of people demonstrating higher scores in the population as a whole. However, in 2008, the trend took a sudden downward turn with the advent of economic difficulties.
- *Gender-related trends*—Gender differences have begun to equalize. Previously, they were heavily skewed in favor of women, who demonstrated superior mastery in all skills except for self-awareness (which was equal).
- *EQ and Career*—Bradberry and Greaves's global study of 500,000 people at all levels of business showed middle management to have the highest scores, with CEOs exhibiting the lowest. No matter what the level, though, those who demonstrated higher EQ scores consistently outperformed their peers.
- *EQ and Age*—EQ improves with age, which at least in part explains the steady increase in EQ with each previous generation.
- *EQ and Culture*—Since some cultures foster emotional and relationship management while others work against it, it stands to reason that certain cultures will have an advantage over others unless similar practices are incorporated.

General Observations

- EQ is trainable and flexible and, therefore, requires regular and consistent cultivation and maintenance.
- EQ is considered the single most influential leadership quality as well as the top ingredient in determining performance in any job.
- EQ being a trainable and flexible skill, the process of learning emotional mastery can be accelerated through early training and practice, thus ensuring the availability of adequate leadership at all times.
- EQ and economic, as well as general well-being, are strongly linked. This is true for both individuals and groups, from organizations to countries.

Key People

Butch Connor (The Power of Emotional Self-Management)

On Memorial Day weekend of 2004, surfer Butch Connor had a harrowing encounter with a great white shark, one of his worst nightmares, during which he experienced a rapid sequence of emotions, including terror, anger, curiosity, despair, resignation, and hope. At one point, Butch realized that the shark was responding to his fear and that he needed to get a handle on his emotions if he was to have a fighting chance of survival. As soon as he made this realization, his body, which had been frozen in panic, responded positively, allowing him to both warn the other surfers and paddle with all his might to the shore. In the process, Butch learned something about his mind, body, and emotions: once he realized that his emotions were governing his body counterproductively, he used his reason to reverse the process—and it worked.

Please note that the "identifying information" of the individuals described in the case studies has been changed by the authors to protect the privacy of those involved. Because of this, names have been included in quotes, as in the original text, and job titles are offered as an approximate guide to understanding the context.

"Dave T." and "Maria M." (Self-awareness)

"Dave T.," a regional service manager, managed his emotions—not the other way around. Dave's communications were clear and honest, and his actions were considered rather than rash or self-centered. He did not hide negative reactions, yet he also did not dwell on negative situations, but took a proactive approach.

"Maria M.," a human resources manager had a similar degree of control over her emotions and reactions. However, control did not preclude honesty, openness, and directness, nor did those qualities preclude kindness.

"Tina J." and "Giles B." (Lack of self-awareness)

"Tina J.," a marketing manager, and "Giles B.," an operations director, both at times lost sight of the effect that they had on other people, usually when they were experiencing strong emotions like excitement or urgency. The result was that they sometimes overwhelmed others or rubbed them the wrong way. The intensity of their personalities, expressed by Tina as urgency, aggressiveness, and sometimes, defensiveness, and by Giles as passion, also resulted in a tendency to miss salient cues relating to other people's needs and attempts to communicate.

"Lane L." and "Yeshe M." (Self-management)

The high-scoring self-management case studies balanced complementary positive characteristics while maintaining a sense of cool and calm in the face of stressful situations. Both "Lane L.," a healthcare administrator, and "Yeshe M.," a computer programmer, demonstrated such qualities as sensitivity and tact without losing their directness and firmness. Both also set themselves high standards of behavior and adhered to them, even when the surrounding mentality was not encouraging.

"Jason L." and "Mei S." (Lack of self-management)

In different ways, both "Jason L.," an IT consultant, and "Mei S.," a regional sales director, demonstrated a lack of control over their emotions or, to put it another way, a lack of thought about how their actions affected their colleagues or team. Jason was prone to emotional outbursts, and Mei was too communicative toward her staff with regard to negative or frustrating administrative situations. She also allowed her own focus, drive, and competitiveness to get in the way of the effective management of her large team.

"Alfonso J." and "Maya S." (Social awareness)

The high-scoring social awareness cases were similar in their active engagement with other people, the difference being that "Alfonso J.," a pharmaceutical sales manager, possessed an outstanding aptitude for reading emotions while "Maya S.," an organizational development executive proved herself to be especially adept at active listening. Both were respectful and engaged in their dealings with others and consequently inspired such feelings as loyalty, uplift, ease, and inspiration.

"Craig C." and "Rachel M." (Lack of social awareness)

A lack of social awareness often results in people feeling that they are not being heard. "Craig C.," an attorney, had a tendency to give too little attention and credence to other people's ideas and plans. Like the other case study, a project manager called "Rachel M.," he would get so focused on his own ideas that he could not hear anything else. In both cases, there were complaints that they didn't slow down sufficiently to listen with both their hearts and minds. Both also had issues communicating their ideas in a way that could maintain interest or gain acceptance. In short, they had difficulty connecting with other people.

"Gail C." and "Allister B." (Relationship management)

The outstanding qualities of both high-scoring case studies in relationship management were empathy and a skillful and consistent approach to handling personal interactions. Both "Gail C.," a chief financial officer, and "Allister B.," a physician, were direct but at the same time sensitive and caring in their dealings, never making the other person feel small or uncomfortable. Though both were also in clear positions of authority, their approach to others, whether staff or patients (in Allister's case), was always supportive, compassionate, and positive.

"Dave M." and "Natalie T." (Lack of relationship management)

In contrast to the high scorers, "Dave M.," a sales manager, and "Natalie T.," a floor supervisor, both left people feeling demeaned because of their careless behavior. Both exhibited a lack of verbal and emotional control, a tendency to be too open with counterproductive, negative opinions, and a lack of either awareness or caring with regard to the impact of their actions and emotions on others. Both also regularly dismissed or ignored other people's ideas or complaints. The result was that people often felt demeaned. In Dave's case, there were also trust issues, biased behavior, and overwhelming or reactive behavior while Natalie was often negative, unsupportive, and unappreciative.

Sheila, Assistant Vice-President (EQ and Gender)

Sheila's intelligence and excellent work quickly put her on the fast track as she moved from her beginnings as a healthcare financial consultant to her position as an assistant vice-president on the way up to the top. But in the eyes of those who observed her, the real reason behind her success was her extraordinary ability to understand and deal with people—her emotional intelligence.

Chapter Summary

Chapter 1

Chapter 1 begins with the harrowing story of Butch Connor's encounter with a great white shark which, as a surfer, was one of his worst nightmares. Butch's goal in paddling away from the other surfers was to relax; instead, his meeting with the shark led him to experience a rapid succession of emotions that included terror, anger, curiosity, despair, resignation, and hope. In large part, the intensity of his emotions controlled his actions: panic caused him to freeze; anger motivated him to get away, and a moment of curiosity coupled with resignation (which was broken by a sudden, violent movement) made him want to touch the shark. At times, his reason would break through his fear, and he would be able to subdue his emotions and direct his body to act more productively. In the midst of being frozen with panic, he had realized that it was his fear that the shark was responding to and that he needed to get a handle on his emotions if he was to have a fighting chance of survival. As soon as he made this realization, his body responded positively, allowing him to both warn the other surfers and paddle with all his might until he reached the shore.

Butch's experience was a lesson in the power of emotion to affect his actions for either better or worse. Bradberry and Greaves explain this through a diagram showing the neural pathway that links the spinal cord with the brain as having to go through the limbic system, or the seat of emotion, before it reaches the prefrontal cortex, the area associated with rational thinking. Greaves and Bradberry describe this link between the reasoning and the feeling parts of the brain as being the physical aspect of emotional intelligence. But Butch learned something else about his mind, body, and emotions: once he realized that his emotions were governing his body counterproductively, he used his reason to reverse the process—and it worked. He had discovered one of the essential elements of emotional intelligence—the ability to manage emotions rather than letting them manage you.

Until recently, EQ has always been eclipsed by IQ, which was thought to be the crucial factor in determining success. Yet studies have revealed that a high IQ accounts for only 20 percent of successes while a high EQ explains an impressive 70 percent. Unlike IQ, though, which Bradberry and Greaves claim to be a fixed learning capacity, EQ can be developed. To this end, the book presents 66 strategies together with an assessment test, both of which are part of a program designed to maximize each individual's emotional intelligence. The assessment test, which is strongly recommended, acts as summary of current individual skills, a learning guide, a memory aid, and a means of measuring progress in what the authors clearly deem a vital and valuable skill.

Chapter 2

Chapter 2 describes the larger picture before delving into the book's details. The authors particularly note the lack of emotional awareness that plagues two-thirds of the world's people, who are unable to either identify, comprehend, or manage their own emotions.

The range of specific emotions that we have to choose from is extensive as illustrated by a chart listing 100 different examples. But according to Bradberry and Greaves, they can all be categorized under five main headings: happiness, sadness, anger, fear, and shame. These are further divided into high, medium, and low degrees of intensity. In part, the aim of the chart is to show us how many emotions we typically experience in one day.

Triggers and Hijackings

The authors define "emotional hijackings" as those instances when our emotions get the better of our thinking and take over our actions, often to our detriment. They cite the example of Butch Connor's paralysis from the fear induced by the great white shark. "Trigger events," on the other hand, are events that produce an extended emotional response.

The Whole Person

The authors distinguish three main aspects of the person: IQ, EQ, and personality. They define IQ as a fundamental ability to learn that remains the same throughout an individual's lifetime. Unlike IQ, EQ can be improved through learning and practice, although some people come by it more naturally than others. Furthermore, there is no correlation between IQ and EQ, which are considered entirely separate skills. The same holds true for personality which, like IQ, is deemed unchanging and separate from emotional intelligence. Personality can be used to help improve EQ, but like IQ, it is not essential to the process. All three together give a more complete picture of the whole person.

EQ and Professional Success

The impact of emotional intelligence on professional success is significant. In studying EQ next to 33 different work-related skills, the authors found that the skills in question could all be included under the EQ heading and that EQ was the single most reliable factor in determining such qualities as excellence and leadership.

The good news is that a low initial EQ score, even when coupled with low work performance, in no way limits a person's ability to excel. Those who work at it can even improve to the extent that they can match their successful colleagues, and since EQ is strongly tied to work performance, earning power, and emotional fulfillment, this may certainly be considered a benefit.

Chapter 3

The Four Skills

In Chapter 3, Bradberry and Greaves introduce us to the fundamental four skills of emotional intelligence. EQ is divided into two main categories: personal and social competence. These are in turn divided into awareness and management of either oneself or others. Specifically, they are called self-awareness, self-management, social awareness, and relationship management.

Case Studies

To bring home these ideas in a concrete manner, the chapter includes case studies of real people with real assessment scores and comments by co-workers. Only their names and "other identifying information" (a probable reference to job titles) have been changed, presumably to protect their privacy. Since many people confuse EQ with charisma, the idea behind the case study section is to give us a sense of what emotional intelligence looks like in action.

Self-Awareness

As the name suggests, "self-awareness" means being aware of and understanding your own positive and negative emotions and reactions. It entails being willing to honestly work through both your feelings and whatever triggers them. In fact, according to the authors, just thinking about self-awareness helps to improve the skill, and because it is such a basic aspect of emotional intelligence, a well-developed self-awareness improves a person's abilities with the other three EQ skills, as well. Finally, being aware of oneself makes a vast difference in both overall personal satisfaction and job performance, a good reason why self-awareness should not be relegated to emergency times, but should include every aspect of our lives.

Self-awareness case studies

Self-awareness in action—The outstanding characteristic in "Dave T.'s" case was that he managed his emotions—not the other way around. Dave's communications were clear and honest, and his actions were considered rather than rash or self-centered. He did not hide negative reactions, yet he also did not dwell on negative situations, but took a proactive approach.

The other high scorer, "Maria M.," had a similar degree of control over her emotions and reactions. However, as in Dave T.'s case, control did not preclude honesty and openness, nor did those qualities in turn preclude kindness. What was striking in both cases was the balance of necessary and beneficial qualities in relation to both themselves and others.

When self-awareness is missing—In "Tina J.'s" and "Giles B.'s" cases, the situation was a little different. Both at times lost sight of their effect on other people, usually when they were experiencing strong emotions like excitement or urgency. The result was that they sometimes overwhelmed other people or rubbed them the wrong way.

What is noteworthy about all of these situations is that, although the authors define "self-awareness" as an awareness of one's own emotions and triggers, the key component in every case above is the individual's awareness (or lack of it) of the effect of his or her actions and words on others.

Self-Management

In brief, self-management refers to the action or restraint that results from self-awareness. It is the ability to steer your life in a positive direction, whether that means managing stressful situations or dealing effectively with temporary uncertainty. An important characteristic of self-management is the ability to defer momentary needs or desires in favor of a larger goal. Those who can do this are more likely to achieve their goals while at the same time maintaining their emotional stability.

Self-management case studies

Self-management in action—The high-scoring self-management case studies are like the self-awareness ones in that they balance complementary positive characteristics while maintaining a sense of cool and calm in the face of stressful situations. Both "Lane L." and "Yeshe M." demonstrated such qualities as sensitivity and tact without losing their directness and firmness. Both also set themselves high standards of behavior and adhered to them, even when the surrounding mentality was not encouraging.

When self-management is missing—In different ways, both "Jason L." and "Mei S." demonstrated a lack of control over their emotions or, to put it another way, a lack of thought about how their actions affected their colleagues or team. Jason was prone to emotional outbursts, and Mei was too communicative toward her staff with regard to negative or frustrating administrative situations, in addition to allowing her own focus, drive, and competitiveness to get in the way of the effective management of her large team.

Noteworthy here is that the high scorers set themselves high standards of behavior while the lower scorers neglected to think as carefully about the importance and impact of their actions and words.

Social Awareness

Like self-awareness, social awareness is what the authors call a "foundational skill," a skill that provides the basis for developing other abilities. Specifically, it is the awareness or accurate perception and understanding of other people's thoughts and emotions. Social awareness means taking enough time away from your own internal activity to truly grasp the inner life of another person without allowing your own preconceptions to interfere.

Social awareness case studies

Social awareness in action—The high-scoring social awareness cases were similar to each other in their active engagement with other people, the difference being that "Alfonso J.'s" outstanding aptitude was to read emotions while "Maya S." proved herself to be especially adept at active listening. Both were respectful and engaged in their dealings with others and consequently inspired such feelings as loyalty, uplift, ease, and inspiration.

When social awareness is missing—Not surprisingly, the lack of social awareness often manifests itself as people feeling that they are not being heard. "Craig C.'s" issue was a tendency to give too little attention and credence to other people's ideas and plans. Like the other case study, "Rachel M.," he would get so focused on his own ideas that he could not hear anything else. In both cases, there were complaints that they did not slow down sufficiently to listen both with their hearts and minds. Both also had issues communicating their ideas in a way that could maintain interest or gain acceptance. In short, they had difficulty connecting with other people.

Relationship Management

Relationship management can be viewed as the culmination all four skills because it utilizes the previous three to effectively manage interactions and relationships. Bradberry and Greaves differentiate between "relationships" and "interactions" according to their frequency—the more frequent the interaction, the more it turns into a relationship. They emphasize the need to manage all interactions, including the difficult or unpleasant ones, since doing so generally enhances genuine communication and aids in resolving conflict and stress. Not least, they see quality relationships as an important aspect of life, something to be cultivated and valued, but at the same time, they recommend adopting the attitude of finding worth in every interaction.

Relationship management in action—The outstanding qualities of the high-scoring case studies in relationship management are empathy and a skillful and consistent approach to handling personal interactions. Both "Gail C." and "Allister B." were direct but at the same time sensitive and caring in their dealings, never making the other person feel small or uncomfortable. Though both were also in clear positions of authority, their approach to others, whether staff or patients (in Allister's case), was always supportive, compassionate, and positive. The reactions from others in both cases were that people felt built up, encouraged, and deeply appreciative.

When relationship management is missing—By contrast, the low scorers in relationship management, "Dave M." and "Natalie T.," both left people feeling demeaned because of their careless behavior. Both exhibited a lack of verbal and emotional control, a tendency to be too open with counterproductive, negative opinions, and a lack of either awareness or caring with regard to the impact of their actions and emotions on others. Both also regularly dismissed or ignored other people's ideas or complaints. The result was that people often felt demeaned. In Dave's case, there were also trust issues, biased behavior, and overwhelming or reactive behavior while Natalie was often negative, unsupportive, and unappreciative.

Chapter 4

Chapter 4 begins by explaining the value of developing your EQ. The authors liken the neural pathways connecting the emotional and rational parts of the brain to a road that benefits from increased traffic. Developing this connection—or growing the road—comes from thinking about and subsequently acting on your emotions. Through deliberate changes in thought and behavior, the brain's "plasticity" allows it to gradually add connections, so that what once was a struggle eventually becomes habitual.

The Emotional Intelligence Action Plan

The book's Emotional Intelligence Action Plan aims to help people develop this connection.

1. The plan begins with taking the *Emotional Intelligence Appraisal* test, which is available

online and requires a passcode (you can find this at the end of the book in an attached envelope). After this, the participant records his or her scores (on page 56 of the book, under My Journey Begins) under the five categories of general emotional intelligence and the four fundamental skills discussed in Chapter 3.

2. Following that, you (or the person in question) are asked to choose one skill at a time to work on since this more concentrated method has been found to be most effective as well as beneficial for learning future EQ skills.

3. Next, you choose and record three strategies related to the selected skill. In both numbers 2 and 3, selections can be made based on individually tailored recommendations generated in response to appraisal test results, or they can be chosen more freely (within the specific category).

4. Select a mentor who is adept at this skill to help guide you and provide feedback as you develop your new ability. This includes meeting regularly as well as writing his or her name in your plan.

5. Mastering the new skill requires a lot of patience and practice, so rehearse your chosen strategies often and expect to wait a few months (from three to six) before seeing permanent change. Also, do not expect perfection; aim instead for success. The authors warn that perfect mastery means that you are not being challenged enough.

6. When you are satisfied with your progress, take the appraisal test again, and then perform the second part of the action plan. This involves listing the new scores next to the old and computing the point differences (+ or -) between them.

Once all of this has been completed, a new skill is chosen, along with three relevant strategies, and the process begins again.

Chapter 5

In this chapter, we learn the fifteen strategies for self-awareness, which the authors define as an in-depth knowledge of our authentic self. Knowing our genuine essence is not something that is achieved quickly or all at once; rather, it is an ongoing process that is accomplished in layers and that requires engaging honestly with both the positive and the negative. Emotions are messages, so not facing them when they emerge is ultimately not only counterproductive but potentially destructive. As difficult as it may be to face our real feelings, doing so is a sign of progress in both self-knowledge as well as the strength of mind and character required to embark on such a journey.

The Fifteen Strategies for Self-Awareness

The rest of the chapter is devoted to outlining the fifteen unassuming yet insightful strategies designed to enhance growth in self-awareness.

1. **Stop labeling your emotions as good or bad**.
   Judging your emotions prevents you from fully

understanding the message they are trying to convey and makes it more difficult to process them. By not suppressing or judging them, you allow the process to unfold and conclude more rapidly. Once your feelings have had a chance to truly speak, they have done their job and can disappear.

2. **Be aware of your emotions' ongoing impact on others.** Bradberry and Greaves call this observing "the ripple effect." People may think that their sudden explosions or outpourings only affect their immediate target, but, in fact, they can create a degree of wariness in those observing (or, presumably, hearing about) the action. The result is a cramping of the feeling of trust and freedom that is necessary for producing the best possible results.

The authors' recommendation is to be attentive to the immediate effects of your emotions on others and to use that as a measure of their ultimate, wider influence. They also recommend thinking carefully about your emotional behavior and questioning others about its effects.

3. **Allow yourself to experience your discomfort.** The authors call this "leaning into your discomfort" so that you genuinely experience it instead of avoiding it. This strategy is similar to the first in that it encourages you to be with the emotion, allowing it to speak rather than sweeping it under the rug. Preventing the emotional experience from fully surfacing merely postpones the event and results in a stunted personal development.

4. **Experience your feelings on a physical level.** To get comfortable with this, Bradberry and Greaves recommend closing your eyes and taking note of your current physiological condition—how fast your heart is beating, which parts of your body are tense, the quality of your breathing, and so on. Once you have done this, think of a positive and a negative experience from your past. As you think of each event separately, notice what types of emotional and physical reactions you are having. Doing this will enable you to recognize the physical symptoms more readily when they occur in your life.

5. **Know your triggers**. This means being aware of which specific people and things set you off. Pinpointing the exact source of your annoyance reduces the chances of being caught off guard, which gives you more control over the situation.

The next recommended step is to delve more deeply into the reasons behind your annoyance. Does the situation remind you of someone or something in your past? Or does it mask some hidden tendency in yourself? Using this strategy does not require overcoming your triggers: the important thing for the moment is to simply become of aware of them and to help with this, the authors recommend keeping a list.

6. **"Watch yourself like a hawk."** This expression usually means to "watch yourself carefully." The authors, however, take the analogy one step further. Their point is that, because a hawk can fly, it has an

overview, giving it a wider vista and, therefore, greater objectivity and predictive ability.

What this means in practice is taking the time to notice your thoughts and emotions before acting on them and then to imagine the larger view from "above." The authors give the example of a parent waiting for his/her teenage son to come home after already breaking his curfew by two hours. Taking a step back from the immediate feelings of anger and frustration allow the parent to see that venting these emotions will not change anything, but being aware of them and their reasons allows the parent to give a more coherent explanation for whatever measures he/she decides to enforce.

7. **Keep a journal.** Keeping a journal of your feelings has elements of some of the other strategies, such as taking a step back to gain more objectivity and watching carefully for trigger events. Writing down your feelings, reactions, and accompanying physical sensations on a daily basis should function as a memory aid, provide you with a reference, and enable you to spot patterns within a month.

8. **Don't let a bad mood fool you.** There are times when a foul mood grips our minds and emotions, coloring our whole world. At these times, we need to be particularly aware so that our perceptions, which after all are only temporary, don't lead us to make poor decisions. Admitting and thinking about our feelings can help things to pass more quickly, although the authors warn us to not spend too much time reflecting on the negative.

9. **Don't let a good mood deceive you, either.** Unfortunately, the high of a good mood is equally capable of leading to poor decision-making as the low of a particularly bad mood. The authors use the common phenomenon of impulsive overspending at a sale as a typical example, the point being that we need to guard against excessive impulsiveness under all conditions in order to avoid remorse.

10. **Question and analyze your actions and emotions.** This means digging deep down to the source and discovering the origins of your actions and feelings, especially if they don't match your regular behavior. This thought process alone of trying to remember who or what first prompted the reactions that now seem to govern you is a key to regaining self-control.

11. **Connect with your values.** The authors maintain that the often hectic pace of our lives keeps us looking outward and that this outward focus makes it easy to lose sight of our deeper ideals, a state that can sometimes lead to regrettable actions. To counteract this, the authors recommend keeping a list on a regular basis (anywhere from daily to monthly). The list should have two columns, one for values and beliefs and the other for any actions taken that run contrary to them. The resulting self-awareness will help us to check in with ourselves before we act.

12. **"Check yourself."** So far, the emphasis has been on connecting with our internal states and thoughts, but in this particular strategy, the authors encourage us to check our external condition since this can function as a manifestation of our internal mood. Our facial expressions as well as how we dress, stand, or wear our hair can indicate a lot about our state of mind; or they can project a

"default" condition that has become habitual. The impression we give, whether of trying too hard or not trying at all, can in large part create the day's mood, so the recommendation is to make sure that it matches the reality before it leaves an unwanted mark on our experience.

13. **Notice your feelings in music, books, movies, and other art forms.** Not everyone has an easy time connecting with or expressing their inner world. If that describes you, observing your reactions to different art forms can provide a clue to your own emotions and mood. When you find yourself responding to some aspect of a book or movie, a piece of music or a work of art, allow yourself to explore the experience further: it may be communicating information about your own deeper thoughts and feelings.

14. **Ask for feedback.** Our self-perception is at best highly subjective, so having the courage and openness to ask for feedback from others can help lead us to a more objective view. This involves gathering a number of different perspectives and then looking for common threads. When requesting feedback, be sure to ask for specific examples.

15. **Learn your personal stress signals.** Symptoms of too much stress can be either physical, emotional, or mental, but in this fast-paced world, they can be easy to miss or ignore when still in their subtle, preliminary stages. The key to preventing a worse situation is to familiarize yourself with your own symptoms—whether a headache, an upset stomach, or various emotional or mental cues—and then heed their advice and take some time for yourself, for what the authors call "[recharging] your emotional battery."

Chapter 6

Self-management is the next step after self-awareness. It is the quality that allows you to manage your emotions rather than the other way around. When self-management is in place, you have the ability to balance your own needs and emotions with the needs and emotions of those around you while still achieving your goals.

The self-management strategies listed in Chapter 6 are straightforward but effective, having been carefully tested and selected to represent different facets of the skill. As the authors say, practicing them daily won't turn your life into a fairy tale, and there will still be trigger moments, but on the whole, you will experience much more control over your life.

The Seventeen Strategies for Self-Management

As in Chapter 5, the remainder of this chapter provides a list of relevant strategies designed to improve the skill in question.

1. **Breathe**. The authors call this section "Breathe Right," since many people's breathing is too shallow to fully meet their needs. The problem is that they don't realize it, having become accustomed to an insufficient intake of air. According to Bradberry and Greaves, the brain requires 20 percent of our air intake, which it then parcels out first to the vital functions and then to the complex functions, such as remaining calm and alert—an obviously crucial self-management skill.

   Adequate breathing means allowing the abdomen to expand on the inbreath, unlike the high chest breathing that is apparently common among many. The strategy, therefore, involves placing one hand on the sternum (the large chest bone) and the other on the diaphragm (stomach area) or lower abdomen (the authors use the word "stomach"). If your abdominal area is expanding more than your chest, then you are breathing correctly.

   As simple as this strategy is, it is extremely effective as a calming technique that shifts the focus toward a more rational, positive outlook, making it an excellent self-management tool.

2. **Write an "Emotions vs. Reasons List."** This strategy is recommended when the emotional and rational parts of your brain are in conflict. Making an Emotions vs. Reason List involves listing your emotional reasoning in one column and your rational thoughts in another. Once you have

completed this, examine the two columns to see how each type of thinking might be interfering with the other. Doing this makes it easier to sort things out and decide which type of decision is more appropriate for the particular situation.

3. **Make an open commitment to your goals.** The authors call this strategy "[Making] Your Goals Public." Making a "public" commitment, even if only with one person (the authors give the example of meeting a running partner every morning), functions as added motivation for achieving your objectives by making others aware of both your goals and your progress. In addition, they recommend that you ask the person or people in question to track your progress and hold you responsible for it, with the added option of meting out a penalty or reward.

4. **Count to ten.** The simple strategy of counting to ten gives the emotional part of your brain time to chill down while the rational part kicks in. The authors recommend taking a deep breath and then silently counting a single number on each exhalation. Even if you don't make it all the way to ten, you will have gained some valuable time to rethink your approach before doing or saying something that you regret or that just creates more problems in the long (or short) run. At times, you will need a cover strategy so that what you're actually doing is not obvious. The authors give the example of one person who always brought a drink to meetings and took a sip when he needed extra time.

5. **Give the dust time to settle.** When we are upset or confused, it's easy to want to rush our decision-making before allowing things to settle and become clear. The authors call this strategy "Sleep On It," and they quote Tolstoy's *War and Peace* as

mentioning the ability of time and patience to bring clarity and healing. So rather than allowing your confusion and upset to rule your thoughts and direct your steps, simply choose to wait for things to settle. As the authors point out, something may even happen during that time to make the situation clearer.

6. **Consult with someone who is adept at self-management.** This strategy involves finding someone who is a talented self-manager, taking him or her out to lunch, and learning the secrets of his/her success, especially in relation to the issues that are most problematic for you. Once you have had a chance to try out a few of the recommended techniques, find out if you can set up another meeting (the authors don't say why, but presumably it's to review your progress and augment your understanding).

If you're uncertain as to who might be a good self-manager, ask the person you have in mind to take the assessment test recommended in the book (the *Emotional Intelligence Appraisal* test). Also, be sure to have him or her review the chapter on self-management before your first meeting.

7. **Put on a happy face.** According to the authors, French university researchers have found that the act of using your smile muscles actually fools the brain into thinking that you're happy. The students in the research study who held a pencil between their teeth while reading the newspaper comics had a more enjoyable time than those who held a pencil

between their lips. Reading a funny book or watching a funny show can also be helpful when a happy face is needed, although the authors don't negate the validity of a difficult mood, since it carries with it an indispensable message.

8. **Set aside problem-solving time.** This does not need to be a lot of time. Fifteen minutes a day is sufficient, but it should be dedicated solely to clearing your head of the many thoughts and feelings that sometimes clutter our days. That means eliminating all distractions to just think. In the authors' opinion, well-planned decisions are usually more successful than those made while you're rushed, harried, or overly emotional.

9. **Manage your self-talk.** "Self-talk" refers to the flow of inner comments that we make to ourselves throughout the day, for better or worse. This becomes more relevant when we recognize the power of our thoughts to influence how we feel both emotionally and physically. It makes sense, therefore, to learn to regulate our thoughts so that they direct our emotions and lives in the most positive way possible. This means becoming conscious of negative self-talk and deliberately making a different, more positive choice.

The authors give three examples of frequent instances of negative self-talk, along with offering some more positive options:

- *"I always ..." or "I never ..."*—Statements like this are obvious exaggerations that attempt to lock you into a negative mode. By changing your statement to "sometimes" or "this time," you recognize that each situation is different, which enables you to examine it from a fresh, rational perspective.

- *Stick to the facts.* Calling yourself "an idiot" when you simply made a mistake is neither accurate nor productive. Focusing on facts instead of judgments will help you to be more objective and proactive.
- *Take responsibility for yourself while avoiding blame.* Constantly blaming either yourself or others is a mind game that leads nowhere. Instead, take responsibility for your own actions, and recognize that others need to be responsible for theirs, as well.

10. **Visualize success.** Our brains have a hard time distinguishing between what we see with our eyes versus what we see with our minds. This makes visualization a particularly powerful tool that can significantly enhance our chances at success and accelerate the development of the neural pathways that solidify a new habit.

One of the best times to practice this is before bedtime. Make sure that your environment is free from distractions. Then first visualize the negative scene or problem as realistically as possible so that it evokes the feelings that are causing you discomfort. Now change your behavior and emotions to positive ones. Practice this every night as a way of solving difficult issues that arise.

11. **Improve your sleep habits.** Not enough quality sleep robs you of the energy that allows you to

remain alert, calm, and flexible, and this, in turn, makes it difficult to manage your emotions. To help your brain access the quality sleep that it needs to recharge adequately, be sure to incorporate the following beneficial habits:

- Allow for twenty minutes of outdoor morning sunlight every day—needed for resetting your internal clock.
- Since computer light mimics sunlight, allow two hours before bedtime away from the computer.
- Use your bed for sleeping only. This conditions your body to respond appropriately at bedtime.
- Avoid or minimize caffeine, and drink it only in the morning. The effects of caffeine decrease by half every six hours, which means that you will still be processing one quarter of your morning intake twelve hours later.

12. **Focus on possibilities, not limitations.** There are times when difficult or negative situational factors are beyond our personal control. However, how we choose to approach the situation is never beyond our control. Also, in most circumstances, there are factors that we can and should control, and it's these that we need to focus on and take responsibility for.

13. **Keep your body and emotions synchronized.** This means keeping your body language and emotions in harmony with each other. But the section also refers to managing both your body and your emotions with your thoughts. The authors give the example of Chelsea "Sully" Sullenberger, the pilot who safely crash-landed a plane in the Hudson River by subduing his fear, maintaining his

physical and emotional equanimity, and focusing on what he needed to do—to land everyone safely. His ability to control himself ensured his success.

14. **Consult with someone who has an objective viewpoint.** When faced with a difficult decision, we can too easily find ourselves going around in the same circles. A fresh, uninvolved perspective can be helpful in such cases. The person you choose should have as little investment in the situation as possible; otherwise, you risk receiving an opinion that is either biased or too much like your own. To avoid this, the authors recommend potentially listening to the opinion of a devil's advocate, even when this might not be what you want to hear.

15. **Learn something valuable from everyone you meet.** How we approach people can make a monumental difference in our experience. Taking the offensive or defensive mode prevents us from learning new things and significantly adds to our stress level. Choosing instead to see everyone as having something valuable to offer allows us to potentially transform every encounter into something beneficial. Even negative situations can hold vital lessons for us when viewed from a positive perspective. At a minimum, we will gain a greater measure of calm, control, and flexibility that can serve us well in any situation.

16. **Schedule mental recharge time.** Because of the positive chemicals it releases into the brain, the authors believe vigorous physical exercise to be the best way to mentally recharge, but gentler exercise such as yoga, gardening, massage, walking in the park, and other relaxing activities are also recommended, both for the body and the mind. Since scheduling recharge time is an issue for

many people, Bradberry and Greaves suggest inserting it at the beginning of the week before life's inevitable events and interruptions squeeze it out. More important, though, is to view it as an essential maintenance task—a regular priority rather than an occasional activity to be included as time permits.

17. **Expect change.** Learning to expect change as inevitable and imminent means that we are more likely to prepare for it instead being caught off guard. Even the things in our lives that seem most stable are apt to change, so being mentally prepared can help mitigate some of the negative reactions that unwanted or unexpected changes sometimes bring. The authors recommend dedicating a little time each week to making a list of possible fundamental changes, their relevant warning signs, and any actions needed to prepare for or respond to them. Whether the changes occur or not, the authors see the exercise as a valuable tool for learning adaptability through mental readiness.

Chapter 7

Social awareness is the ability to pick up on cues from other people through such aspects as body language, facial expression, and tone of voice. It is the ability to key into people's emotions, and it has been found to be remarkably consistent across different cultures. To do this effectively requires being both present and clear as well as having an outwardly directed focus that enables you to imagine another person's or group's feelings.

The Seventeen Strategies for Social Awareness

The strategies listed below are designed to aid in removing any blocks to social awareness by helping you to recognize the pivotal signals:

1. **Use people's names when greeting them**. Bradberry and Greaves see our names as an essential part of our identities, which makes greeting someone by name as powerful a technique as it is straightforward. Focusing on remembering a person's name and then using it in conversation or greeting has the ability to both heighten your social attentiveness and make the person feel special.

Don't be discouraged if you have difficulty remembering names. Practice makes perfect. Also, if the name is unclear to you, having the person spell it for you will make it that much easier to recall.

2. **Observe people's body language.** This strategy stresses body language as a clue to a person's real thoughts and feelings and then reduces body language observation to a miniature science. Readers are instructed to notice small signs and shifts in a person's eyes, smile, and overall body posture and movement. For example, are the person's movements relaxed or nervous, slouched or upright? To prove their point, the authors cite the superior ability of professional poker players to analyze these small hints since their success or failure is after all the key to their livelihood.

3. **Pay careful attention to timing.** The authors take this one step further, calling this strategy "Make Timing Everything." What they are referring to is the natural sensitivity that appraises a situation before making a move. Examples include knowing not to approach someone who is in a lousy mood or not asking a business question when someone is obviously upset over a personal issue. The authors are not suggesting manipulation but the human sensitivity that springs from empathy.

To practice this strategy, the authors recommend timing whatever question you plan ask by focusing on the other person's state rather than on your own. With a little sensitivity and compassion, even imperfectly timed questions can sometimes be introduced after first acknowledging and demonstrating concern for the other person's current feelings and needs.

4. **Prepare a "back-pocket question."** This is a question that you pull out of your back pocket (figuratively, of course) in those awkward moments when the conversation threatens to lapse into an uncomfortable silence. The question should be structured to invite more than a one- or two-word response. The authors recommend a "What do you think of ..." format that avoids, however, broaching such subjects as politics or religion.

The purpose of these questions is to bring some life to the conversation, so Bradberry and Greaves's counsel is to not worry if the question seems like a sudden change of subject. However, there will be times when, in spite of your efforts, you simply won't have much luck, and your best option will be to find a way to graciously widen the conversational circle or excuse yourself.

5. **Refrain from taking notes in meetings.** According to the authors, note-taking, like other types of

multitasking, prevents us from paying careful attention to the events taking place in front of us. While taking notes in meetings may be useful in some ways, it may also distract our attention from small clues that provide the key to a fuller understanding of the situation. To pick up on these cues, we need to observe the other people in the room with greater awareness and attention. The strategy, therefore, recommends refraining from note-taking and instead observing people's expressions and making eye contact with each speaker. Your increased focus on your surroundings should help you to capture nuances that you might otherwise miss when your attention is buried in your notes.

6. **Plan ahead for social events.** Social events can be just as nerve-racking or distracting as business events, so doing a bit of planning can relieve your mind and ease the tension. Bradberry and Greaves recommend taking an index card with a few notes that will serve as reminders of salient points that you want to remember to do or say while there. Using this basic device will allow you to accomplish your goals without worrying about having to remember or stressing because you forgot. As a result, you can be more present and truly enjoy yourself.

7. **Clear out the inner clutter.** Social awareness requires clarity, and clarity requires doing away with the incessant mental chatter that can clog our ability to receive information. We either altogether block the outside world, or we color the information we receive with our own preconceptions, often interrupting the other person before giving him or her a chance to finish. Some simple remedies for counteracting these tendencies are: 1. not

interrupting; 2. stopping any planned response before it comes out; and 3. focusing our attention on the person's expressions and on the conversation. As we shift the attention from our own ideas to learning from others, we will hone our listening skills and quiet our minds.

8. **Be in the present.** Being in the present moment, without the distraction of thoughts about the past or the future, enables us to fully experience life. The authors affirm that contemplating the past and mapping out the future are essential activities, but they have their place and should not interfere with our experience of the present. The exercise, therefore, consists in being truly present in each situation and not allowing our minds to wander elsewhere.

9. **Tour your workplace.** The purpose of this exercise is to counteract the tendency to focus on the destination rather than on the journey of life. The "destination" need not be large; it can refer to the smaller daily and hourly goals and schedules that we set for ourselves: the next appointment, the next task, and so on. To switch the focus from destination to journey, the authors recommend two 15-minute tours a week for one month to observe different things that often escape our notice. Dedicate the first tour to taking in small details and the second to moods. Avoid judging what you see while touring. Instead, just observe.

10. **Learn about EQ from movies.** Movies are a terrific way to hone your EQ skills since they are largely about emotional interactions—both positive and negative. Beyond that, you have the advantage of not being directly involved with the characters, which makes it easier to be objective. To hone your skills, this strategy recommends watching two

movies in the coming month. Pay specific attention to how body language relates to emotion, and observe the characters' methods of resolving their conflicts. The authors also recommend rewinding after you have a better understanding of the situation so that you can look for any hints you might have missed the first time.

11. **Listen.** Believe it or not, this takes practice, and according to the authors, it is a dying art. "Listening" also means more than just taking in the words a person is using: it also requires observing the tone, undertone, subtext, speed, and volume that are being used. The practice strategy is, therefore, simply a matter of listening with 100 percent focus. That means no distractions or multitasking and no interruptions. Doing this should increase your awareness of the subtle non-verbal messages that often accompany someone's words.

12. **People-watch.** For this strategy, the authors recommend going to a coffee shop to watch people's movements and interactions from a distance. Like watching movies, doing this enables you to observe without being directly involved so that you can take your time to notice things that you might otherwise be too distracted to pick up on.

13. **Know and understand the cultural rules.** This strategy has become especially relevant in our increasingly multicultural world. Different cultures (and even subcultures) have different rules and expectations. As the authors point out, this includes not only ethnic or national culture but also business and family cultural values and behaviors. Understanding these rules means observing more carefully than usual as well as asking questions to

determine other people's cultural preferences and habits and how they would like to be treated.

14. **Test the accuracy of your observations by asking questions.** Gaining social awareness sometimes means testing your perceptions for accuracy. Asking questions is the easiest way to do this. If people's body language seems out of sync with their statements about how they are doing, you can verify this by asking a sensitively worded question about the discrepancy. Similarly, if someone drops hints without directly saying what he or she is thinking, you can confirm your observations with a simple question.

15. **See things as they do.** The authors call this "[stepping] into their shoes." It is something that actors do naturally, often reporting greater appreciation of even a difficult character's personality. Learning to do this can help to prevent regrets later on, and it's as easy as asking yourself what you would do or say if you were the person in question. To figure this out, consider the person's history in similar situations, being careful to resist the temptation to let any preconceived behavioral notions interfere. Assuming you're comfortable enough with the person, you can then choose an appropriate time to verify your perceptions by asking questions.

16. **Use a 360-survey to get the big picture about yourself.** This means consulting not just those who like you, but those who have issues with you, as well. Their opinions might not be what you want to hear, but they may alert you to potential problems—views that people hold of you that might interfere with the progress of your career. The best way to do this is through a 360-degree survey (an anonymous survey administered to

everyone in your immediate working environment) on the four basic EQ skills. According to the authors, others' viewpoints of us are usually more accurate than our own and can, therefore, give us valuable information about ourselves.

17. **Practice sensing the mood of an entire room.** Rooms usually develop a definite feel based on the collective thoughts, actions, and emotions of the people in them. The number of people and their general purpose for being there can easily influence its overall mood. The authors use the comparison of a convention of networking entrepreneurs versus a roomful of potential jurors awaiting a decision about whether they have been selected for duty, or you might compare Grand Central Station to a wake at a funeral home for a more extreme difference in energies.

The authors recommend two ways to go about practicing this skill, which they consider the culmination of social awareness skills. The first is to use your gut instincts coupled with your observation of people's movements, groupings, and overall energy. The second is to accompany someone with talent and experience in this skill. At first, you can compare notes about your observations, eventually trying it on your own.

Chapter 8

Relationship management represents the final development in learning emotional intelligence skills since it combines and adds to the previous three. As the authors point out, managing relationships is often easy at first, but doing so long-term requires work, patience, and skill, no matter how good the basis of the relationship.

The Seventeen Strategies for Managing Relationships

The following seventeen strategies focus on developing the skills needed in managing relationships so that you can fully enjoy this rewarding, though often challenging, aspect of life:

1. **Maintain an open and curious attitude in relation to others**. No matter how many or few

people we work or socialize with, relationships are a part of life that few of us can escape. Learning how to navigate them effectively is, therefore, a useful skill for most of us. To this end, the authors recommend openness and curiosity as two essential qualities for cultivating good relationships. They define "openness" as the willingness to impart information about yourself to others, one of the benefits being that you are less likely to be misunderstood. The complement to this is curiosity, or interest in other people's thoughts and stories. Like openness, curiosity helps to prevent misunderstanding and ensure that everyone's needs are met. Be sure, however, to use sensitivity when asking and timing your questions. An interested, open-minded approach will get you much further than a judgmental one that implies criticism of the person's choices. Aside from helping you to learn about the person, a friendly curiosity makes others feel appreciated. Regardless of the nature and status of your current relationships, the authors recommend practicing these two qualities several minutes a day with different people.

2. **Build on your natural style of communicating**. We all have ways of communicating that are specific to our own style, though this may vary with the situation. Qualities may range from shy to gregarious, exuberant to ornery, direct to evasive, entertaining to dull, and so on.

Practicing this strategy involves first determining your overall natural style, as observed by you and described by friends, family, and co-workers. Write this at the top of the page (you can choose any adjective you like). Then divide the page into two columns, noting the positive elements of your style on the left side and the negatives on the right (you should evaluate these according to the reactions you have experienced from others). The final step is to honestly decide how to build on the good while eradicating or downplaying the negative elements.

3. **Don't give mixed signals**. This translates into making sure that your body language, expressions, and words match; otherwise, your mixed signals will produce confusion. There are times, however, when allowing your emotions to surface unimpeded is counterproductive, and in those cases, your self-management skills should enable you to govern yourself until you can find a more appropriate moment to broach the subject and express your feelings. Whatever your timing, be sure to choose it so as to produce the best outcome. If you find this impossible to do, then explain the reason or context for the emotion. To practice this strategy, the authors recommend a month of close self-observation, coupled with a concerted effort to maintain synchrony between the different facets of your verbal and physical expression.

4. **Don't forget the power of courtesy**. Courtesy is a social skill that seems to have gone by the wayside in our fast-paced society. Bradberry and Greaves

point out that terms that once were an essential aspect of cultural interaction, such as "please," "thank you," and "I'm sorry," have all, but disappeared from our vocabulary. Yet the simple insertion of one of these at the right moment can have a significant impact on a person's sense of well-being. The strategy, therefore, emphasizes reintroducing habitual good manners into our daily lives, thereby potentially lifting others' spirits as well as our own.

5. **Learn and grow from feedback**. Feedback, even if we don't agree with it, is intended to help us improve; so learning to accept it graciously and evaluate it as objectively as possible is a useful skill to develop. The first step—the receiving step—involves listening carefully, clearing up any questions, and thanking the source of the feedback for at least taking the time to give it. The second step involves absorbing and understanding the message. Resist creating an action plan under pressure; instead, take your time to truly understand. The authors recommend the Emotion vs. Reason list for this step. The third step is to decide what to do. Acting on the feedback gives the other person confidence that he or she has been heard, which in turn benefits the relationship.

6. **Build trust.** Trust is one of the most critical aspects of a relationship, and it often presupposes the presence of a certain amount of it to create more. Trust also takes time to build: you don't need to bare all in one sitting. You do need, however, to be aware of your own requirements, in addition to tuning into and, if necessary, asking the other person about his or hers. Some qualities to keep in mind for building and maintaining trust are openness, sharing, consistency, and dependability.

7. **Maintain an "open-door" policy.** This means allowing for unscheduled meetings with any person at any level without spreading yourself thin. How this works in practice varies with each individual and requires self-management, awareness of others, and a consistent approach that is clearly communicated. Its value is that it imparts a sense of respect and worth and encourages mutual learning.

8. **Manage your anger proactively.** Used wisely at the right time, in the right situation, and for the right reasons, anger can actually be a constructive emotion. Overusing or misusing it can, however, lead to ineffectiveness, like the boy who cried "Wolf!" being ignored by the villagers, who finally got fed up with his games. Anger management is generally not required on a daily basis, so mastering it as a skill may take a little more time and planning when it is needed. Remember: the deciding factor in using this skill should be its potential benefit to the relationship.

9. **Don't run from unavoidable situations.** Sometimes we have no choice, but to deal with someone we would rather avoid. In such cases, we need to use our self- and social awareness skills to make the most of the situation, keeping in mind the common goal as the important element in the relationship. In a close working situation, the starting point is to learn about the person's preferences and experience relative to the job. Explaining your own work preferences (not your feelings about the person) as a next move will help you devise a mutual plan about how to work together. Observe the other person during this process to determine any uncomfortable emotions on his or her part, since this sort of information can be instructive when trying to maneuver a difficult

relationship. Finally, acknowledge your mutual achievement.

10. **Acknowledge other people's emotions.** This means recognizing the validity of other people's feelings, even if you don't agree with them or they make you uncomfortable. In the latter case, the authors recommend "leaning" into your discomfort. Dismissing, exaggerating, or trivializing another's emotions does not help to make the person feel better while recognizing them with even a small gesture shows caring. The simple act of listening and summarizing the person's statements can go a long way toward improving the situation.

11. **Complement feelings or situations in close interactions.** The word "complement" as used here by the authors does not refer to mirroring whatever situation or set of emotions you find yourself dealing with; rather, it means adjusting yourself to the mood or circumstances in a way that is helpful toward solving the issue at hand. To practice this, the authors recommend first thinking back on a situation where someone did or did not complement an obvious mood of yours. How did his or her actions influence the situation and your mood? Once you have reviewed the situation, make a note to complement those close to you—whether friends, family, or co-workers—in a way that is sensitive and helpful.

12. **Show that you care.** When you feel gratitude or appreciation, or if something is important to you, show it. As the authors point out, there is a lot of excellent work going on around us all the time, so take a moment to show your genuine appreciation. Even small gestures, when they come from the heart, can lift someone's spirits and improve

morale, which in turn inspires more good work and a stronger relationship.

13. **Explain your decisions.** Explaining your decisions goes a long way toward helping others to understand and accept them. Not knowing why something is happening or being insufficiently informed can make people uneasy while keeping an open line of communication shows caring, support, and respect. To practice this, look over the decisions you will need to make in the next three months; then list the people they will impact and in what ways. This will give you added insight into others' viewpoints so that you can tailor your explanations of how and why the decisions are being made.

14. **Give honest, constructive feedback.** Giving genuinely constructive feedback involves the use of all four EQ skills and should be viewed as a way of building the relationship. The process breaks down as follows:

- *Self-awareness*—Determine whether or not you feel comfortable giving the feedback along with the reasons for your feelings.

- *Self-management*—Decide how to overcome or deal with any issues discovered during your self-evaluation process.

- *Social awareness*—For feedback to be as constructive as possible, it needs to include your opinion as well as problem-solving suggestions, and it needs to be tailored to the individual. As the examples in the book point out, someone who is direct will require a different approach from someone who is sensitive.

- *Relationship management*—Once you have gone over the feedback with the person take some time to hear his or her viewpoint. Finally, be sure to thank the person for being open to reviewing your recommendations.

15. **Match intention with impact.** Sometimes our intentions just don't translate into the impact that we wanted to produce. We say the wrong thing at the wrong time, even though the intention was positive. The first step toward correcting this situation is to analyze it in detail: write down what you intended, what you did, and the effect it had. Then note what you missed at the time and what you have learned since then, finishing with how you would change your behavior to bring it in line with your intended result.

16. **Offer a way of fixing things if the conversation starts to break down.** The authors call this a "fix-it statement," which can be anything from empathizing with the person's emotions to offering a practical way of repairing the damage, whether perceived or actual. They give the example of airline agents, who typically have a lot of "fix-it" conversations to keep their customers happy. Remember when dealing with this type of situation that what went wrong and why it's less valuable than finding a solution to the problem. In other words, avoid blame, and try to see the situation from the perspectives of all involved. Doing this will help you stay open to listening and communicating, which will facilitate finding an appropriate solution.

17. **Use positive steps when dealing with difficult conversations.** Difficult conversations can be tough to manage, so the authors outline a few constructive steps to ease the process:
    - *Begin on common ground*—Since the conversation promises to be challenging, start with one or more unifying points, even if this

simply means acknowledging and empathizing with the other person's feelings. Do what you can to acknowledge the positive aspects of the relationship, such as valuing the person's work.

- *Listen to the other person's side*—Give the person a chance to speak and feel heard. Not feeling heard causes frustration.
- *Avoid "comebacks"*—Planning your answers prevents you from listening, so again, allow the person to express his or her feelings and thoughts, and avoid becoming defensive.
- *Explain your viewpoint*—This is the part where you explain your feelings, actions, and thoughts in a clear, direct, simple, and empathetic manner. A clear, but sensitive explanation will help the other person to feel better about the situation.
- *Bring the conversation ahead*—At this point, the conversation needs to turn toward a solution that is helpful to the requirements of all parties. In the authors' example of an employee who had been passed over for a promotion, that meant expressing appreciation for the person's work as well as interest in developing her skills further, followed by asking for her input.
- *Keep communicating after the conversation is over*—Tough conversations imply tough situations, which require more than the usual amount of care to ensure a good outcome. What that means in practical terms—for example, scheduling formal or informal meetings—will vary with each situation, but be sure to establish some sort of ongoing communication to make sure that things are progressing in a positive direction.

The authors conclude by pointing out that if you can successfully implement the above strategies and avoid a defensive stance, a difficult interaction can actually present an opportunity for building a stronger relationship.

Chapter 9

TalentSmart® is Travis Bradberry and Jean Greaves's emotional intelligence training, consulting and testing agency that administers the *Emotional Intelligence Appraisal®* test. Their position as leaders in the field has given them the chance to observe the progress of hundreds of thousands of individuals at all career levels. In addition, they have taken an interest in the patterns and shifts in larger EQ trends, such as overall implications for health, happiness, career success, and earnings potential; differences and similarities between the generations and the sexes; and the influence of culture.

Overall Trends in Emotional Intelligence

In their study of changes in emotional intelligence in the US population, Bradberry and Greaves noticed not only an upward trend in the people they tested and instructed, but also in the population as a whole. From 2003 to 2007, there was a steady increase in both average worker EQ as well as an overall increase in the number of favorable scores, which climbed from 13.7 to about 18.3 percent of the population. As the authors point out, those four percentage points represent millions of people. At the same time, there was a significant decrease (17 percentage points) in the number of people with low EQ. This was mitigated somewhat in 2008, when the recession hit the country, but the most significant point was that the overall positive progress was occurring without prior EQ knowledge or testing in the new sample group. The authors drew two main conclusions from the data: that EQ was affected somewhat by troubling circumstances; and that it was infectious—that the behavior of those around us tends to influence our own behavior regardless of whether we have been consciously trained in the same direction.

EQ and Gender

In 2003, Bradberry and Greaves's research showed a significant discrepancy between men and women in emotional intelligence skills. In all but one category—self-awareness, in which their scores were equal—women outperformed men in their mastery of emotions and relationships. Since then, however, the EQ scores of the different sexes have grown closer as men learn to manage and attend to their emotions as a useful part of their decision-making process. Bradberry and Greaves found that most of the best male decision makers also ranked high in emotional intelligence, contradicting the notion that good decision-making skills ignore the emotions.

EQ and Career Level

After testing 500,000 people at all levels of business across the globe, Bradberry and Greaves noticed a steady climb in EQ scores that peaked with middle management and then plummeted until it reached the group with the lowest scores, the CEOs. Yet, regardless of the fact that top executives spend less time managing people, those with higher EQs still exceeded their colleagues in performance. In fact, EQ is considered the single most powerful leadership quality as well as the top ingredient in determining performance in any job.

EQ and Age Differences

In studying the four generations that ranged from the Traditionalists and Baby Boomers to Generations X and Y, it seemed at first glance that there was a correlation between succeeding generations and their capacity for self-management: the younger the generation, the less control people had over managing their emotions. This did not bode well for the workforce—in particular its leadership—since Baby Boomers are in the process of retiring in large numbers. But further examination revealed that the correlation had more to do with the maturity that comes with age than any peculiarity pertaining to the different generations, and since EQ is an improvable skill, that means that the younger generation can accelerate its improvement in self-management ability through training and practice, thus providing the nation's infrastructure with the leadership that will be needed to fill the gap left by the exiting Baby Boomers.

EQ and Cultural Influences

In 2005, TalentSmart® decided to investigate what was behind China's emergence as a knowledge leader in the global market. Using the *Emotional Intelligence Appraisal*® to test 3000 senior executives in their own language, they discovered that although American and Chinese executives scored similarly in self-awareness and social awareness, the Chinese scored fifteen points higher in self-management and relationship management. In other words, they were putting their self- and social awareness to use while American senior managers preferred to simply pay lip service to implementing the same ideas. The authors mention, for example, that Chinese managers regularly take the time to discuss business, career goals, and family issues with their employees over dinner. They are also held—and hold themselves—to the same high standards of behavior that they expect of their workers. As the authors point out, what this information suggests is that emotional intelligence and economic well-being are strongly linked, which means that cultures that emphasize emotional and relationship management skills will have a natural advantage.

Conclusion

Just as entire cultures benefit from the cultivation of emotional intelligence, so, too, can individuals, companies, families, and other groups. But the authors warn that EQ skills need to be actively maintained—that they can be unlearned as well as learned and improved. A stressful situation or a discouraging environment can have a detrimental effect that needs to be guarded against by conscious, habitual practice of EQ skills. Given the strong connection between EQ and prosperity, those who neglect to do this run the risk of decreasing their overall quality of life—economically, personally, and professionally.

About BookCaps

We all need refreshers every now and then. Whether you are a student trying to cram for that big final, or someone just trying to understand a book more, BookCaps can help. We are a small, but growing company, and are adding titles every month.

Visit www.bookcaps.com to see more of our books, or contact us with any questions.

Made in the USA
Lexington, KY
29 April 2013